VOICES IN LITERATURE

BRONZE

Student Journal and Activity Book

Mary Lou McCloskey • Lydia Stack

Heinle & Heinle Publishers • An International Thomson Publishing Company • Boston, Massachusetts 02116 U.S.A.

The publication of *Voices in Literature* was directed by the members of the Heinle & Heinle Middle School, Secondary, and Adult ESL Publishing Team.

Editorial Director: Roseanne Mendoza
Senior Production Services Coordinator: Lisa McLaughlin
Market Development Director: Ingrid A. Greenberg

Also participating in the publication of the program were:

Publisher: Stanley Galek
Senior Assistant Editor: Sally Conover
Manufacturing Coordinator: Mary Beth Hennebury
Production Editor: Maryellen Eschmann Killeen
Compositor: Frank Weaver

Cover art: Michio Takayama, *Gate of Toledo,* circa 1972–78

Manufactured in the United States of America.

ISBN: 0-8384-7032-7

Heinle & Heinle is a division of International Thomson Publishing, Inc.

Contents

Unit 3: Messages

Unit 5: Peace

Student Journal Resource Pages

UNIT

1

Patterns

(Activity Master 1)   *Use with student text page 4.*

Find the Pattern

What comes next?

1, 2, 3, 4, _____ $^1/_8$ $^3/_8$ $^5/_8$ _____

ab   cd   ef _____   ✕ ✖ ✖ ✕ ✕ ✖ ✕ ✖ ✖ _____

/.   //..   ///...   //...   ////.... _____   ↑ ↓ ← → ↑ _____

3, 6, 9, 12, _____   → ⇒ ← _____

1, 1, 2, 3, 5, 8, 13, _____   ☺ ☺☺ ☹ ☺☺ _____

A Z B Y C X _____ _____   . ☐ ◆ ☐ ◆ ☐ _____ _____

Sun, Tues, Thurs, Sat, Mon, _____, _____   1 ! 2 @ 3 # _____ _____
                                                   (Hint: Look at a computer keyboard.)

a e i o u o i _____ _____   1/4, 1, 5/4, 1, 9/4, 1, _____, _____

1o 2 2t 3 3 3t 4 4 4 4f _____   a C e G i K _____ _____

10, 7, 4, _____   A B c d e F G H i j k l _____

Everybody Loves Saturday Night

Everybody Loves Saturday Night
Traditional

English: Everybody loves Saturday night.
Everybody loves Saturday night.
Everybody, everybody, everybody,
everybody.
Everybody loves Saturday night.

Czech: Kazder mah rahd Saotoo vyecher.

Ebo (Spoken in Nigeria):   Onye obula fura SN nanya.

French: Tout le monde aime samedi soir.

German: Wir lieben alle Samstag abend.

Haitian: Tout moun renmen samdi swa.

Hungarian: Mundenkee Serret Sumbut Eshteh.

Italian: Tutti ama Sabato sera.

Japanese: Dá re demo do yó bi gasukí.

Khmer (Spoken in Cambodia):   Tang og ka nia jo jet rea tre tha ngai Sao.

Laotian: Tuk tuk khon mak kuen wan sao.

Lithuanian: Visih melih soobatos vakarra.

Mandarin: Ren ren shi huan li pai loo.

Polish: Kazdeh loobya sabaute vietcher.

Portuguese: Todos gostan dos sabados a noite.

Russian: Vysem nrávit soobohta vyecheram.

Sierra Leone: Mawfay moni s'mah ha bekay.

Singhalese: Samadana sanasurade vakarra.

Slovenian: Kazhday lubee sobautu nautz.

Spanish: A todos les gusta la noche del sábado.

Turkish: Herkes cumartese gecesini sever.

Vietnamese: Ay cung thung nghay thu bay.

Yiddish: Yeder ener glächt [hot lieb] shabbas ba nacht.

Yoruba (Spoken in Nigeria):   Bobo waro ferro Satodeh.

Note: Several of the above are phonetic spellings.

Writing: Your Favorite Day

1. In the box below, draw a picture of your favorite day.

2. Label all the people, objects, and activities in your picture. Use a picture dictionary, translation dictionary, and other people to help you.

3. Write about your picture.

_____

_____

_____

_____

_____

_____

_____

Use with student text pages 9–10.

Chants

In the box below is a counting chant in English. Can you think of others? Can you think of counting chants in another language?

One, two, buckle my shoe; *Three, four, shut the door;* *Five, six, pick up sticks;* *Seven, eight, lay them straight;* *Nine, ten, a big fat hen.*	**Write your counting chant:**

Below is a chant for choosing a leader. Everyone puts one hand in the middle. Touch one hand as you say each number, going around the group. Whoever is touched as you say "more" is out. Continue until only one person is left. That person will be the leader in the game.

One potato, two potato, three potato, four, *Five potato, six potato, seven potato, more.*	**Write a game chant you know:**

In schools, we often use chants to cheer on our teams. The following chant is a school cheer.

Two bits, four bits, six bits, a dollar. *All for our team, stand up and holler.*	**Write a cheer from your school.**

Use with student text pages 14–15, 156.

Writing with a Storyboard

1.	2.	3.
First,	Second,	Third,

4.	5.	6.
Fourth,	Fifth,	Finally,

Use after student text page 15.

Write about a topic you choose.

_____

_____

_____

_____

_____

_____

_____

_____

_____

_____

_____

_____

_____

_____

_____

_____

_____

_____

_____

_____

(Activity Master 5)

Use with student text page 16.

Months Roundtable

1. Work with three other students.
2. Pass the chart around the group.
3. Write something in one box of the chart each time it comes to you.

THE MONTHS							
Month	Name in Another Language	What I Think of	Picture or Symbol	Month	Name in Another Language	What I Think of	Picture or Symbol
January	*enero*	eating menudo on New Year's Day		July			
February				August			
March				September			
April				October			
May				November			
June				December			

(Activity Master 6)

Use with student text page 17.

Where Were You Born?

1. Work in a group of about four.
2. Find where you were born.
3. Help everyone in the group label that place on their maps.
4. Find the place where you live now.
5. Tell your group about the weather during one month of the year in both places. Use some of the words at the bottom of the page. You might use sentences such as these:

    "In *January* in *Eritrea* it is *very warm and sunny*."
    "In *January* in *Toronto* it is *very cold and snowy*."

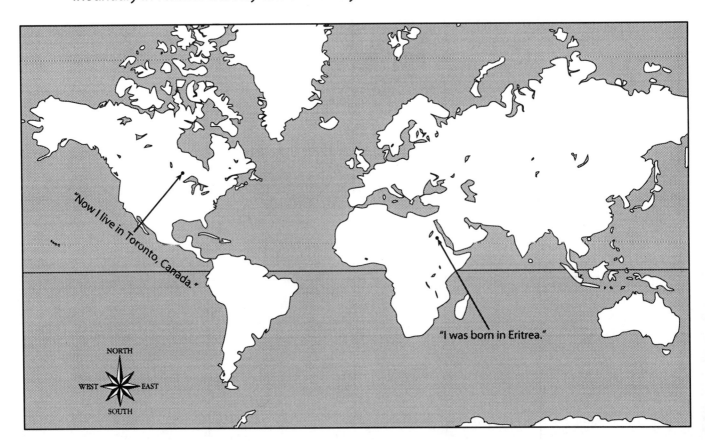

 Hot   **Cold**   **Warm**   **Rainy**   **Snowy**   **Dry**   **Windy**   **Humid**    **Sunny**

Seasons Chart

SEASONS CHART		
Country	**Season**	**Months**

Writing:
Your Favorite Month/Shape Poem

Your Favorite Month:
Write about your favorite month.

My favorite month is _____ because _____

_____

_____

_____

_____

_____

Shape Poem:
Write your own shape poem.

1. Write the words on scrap paper.
2. Draw the shape in pencil in the box below.
3. Write the words on the shape.
4. Share your poem with classmates.

Concentration

1. Cut out the cards on Activity Masters 8 and 9.
2. Play "Concentration" with the picture and/or word cards.
3. You must read the word or name the picture of the cards you match.

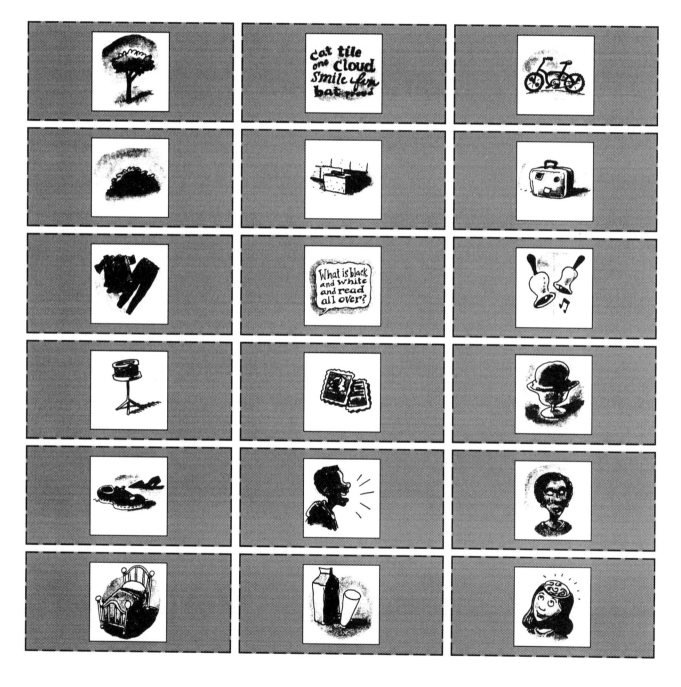

Concentration

Tree	Words	Bike
Bush	Cinder Block	Suitcase
Clothes	Riddle	Bells
Drum	Stamps	Ice Cream
Shoes	Talking	Crying
Bed	Milk	Thinking

Use with student text pages 26–27.

Questions and Answers

Most questions begin with one of these question words:

Who?   What?   When?   Where?   Why?   How?

Others begin with:

Do/Does?   Can?   Will?

1. Work with a partner.
2. Think up questions about the poem. Use the patterns below to help you.
3. Ask your partner questions about the poem.
4. Answer your partner's questions.
5. Take turns asking and answering.
6. Fill in the blanks with your favorite questions and answers. Write others on the back.

a.   **Q:** What is a _____ for?   **A:** A _____ is for
     _____.

b.   **Q:** Do you have a (any) _____?   **A:** (A) _____? _____.
                                                  [yes, no, of course, I think so, maybe]

c.   **Q:** Do you like _____?   **A:** _____.
                                                  [yes, no, of course, I think so, maybe]

d.   **Q:** When do you like to _____?   **A.** I like to _____ when
     _____.

e.   **Q:** Why? (Why not?)   **A:** I like (don't like) to _____
                                                  because _____.

f.   **Q:** Where do you keep your _____? **A:** I keep my _____
                                                  in _____ _____.

g.   **Q:** How do you ride a _____?   **A:** I _____.

h.   **Q:** Who do you _____ with?   **A:** I like to _____ with
     _____.

i.   **Q:** What do you do when you're _____? **A:** When I'm _____, I
     _____.

What Is It For?

1. Work with three other students.
2. Use the pattern below.
3. On the lines below, draft uses for the objects that people in your group brought to class.

_____ is for _____

_____ is for _____

_____ is for _____

_____ is for _____

_____ is for _____

_____ is for _____

Check to make sure that each line starts with a capital letter and ends with a period.

4. Choose the best lines from your group.
5. Arrange your lines into a poem.
6. Write the poem below.

_____

_____

_____

_____

_____

_____

_____

_____

_____

Line Story Storyboard

"When I First Came to This Land" is a *line story.* Each time you tell the story or sing the song, you add a new line. Make a storyboard for the story. Make a storyboard for other line stories or songs.

STORYBOARD FOR "WHEN I FIRST CAME TO THIS LAND"
I called my shack, "Break My Back."
And I called my farm, "_____."   *I called my shack, "Break My Back."*

(Activity Master 14)   *Use with student text page 35.*

"When I First Came to This Land"

Repetition is the use of words, sounds, or phrases over and over again.
A *stanza* is a part, or section, of a poem.

Directions:
Underline the new words in each *stanza*. Notice which words or phrases are repeated. What is the effect of this repetition?

When I First Came to This Land—*Traditional German-American Folk Poem*

When I first came to this land,
I was not a wealthy man.
I got myself a shack.
And I called that shack "Break My Back,"
And the land was sweet and good,
And I did what I could.

When I first came to this land,
I was not a wealthy man.
I got myself a farm.
And I called my farm "Muscle in My Arm,"
And I called my shack "Break My Back,"
And the land was sweet and good,
And I did what I could.

When I first came to this land,
I was not a wealthy man.
I got myself a wife.
And I called my wife "Love of My Life,"
And I called my farm "Muscle in My Arm,"
And I called my shack "Break My Back,"
And the land was sweet and good,
And I did what I could.

When I first came to this land,
I was not a wealthy man.
I got myself a cow.
And I called that cow "No Milk Now,"
And I called my wife "Love of My Life,"
And I called my farm "Muscle in My Arm,"
And I called my shack "Break My Back,"
And the land was sweet and good,
And I did what I could.

When I first came to this land,
I was not a wealthy man.
I got myself a son.
And I called that son "Lots of Fun,"
And I called that cow "No Milk Now,"
And I called my wife "Love of My Life,"
And I called my farm "Muscle in My Arm,"
And I called my shack "Break My Back,"
And the land was sweet and good,
And I did what I could.

When I first came to this land,
I was not a wealthy man.
I got myself a tree.
And I called that tree "Family Tree,"
And I called that son "Lots of Fun,"
And I called that cow "No Milk Now,"
And I called my wife "Love of My Life,"
And I called my farm "Muscle in My Arm,"
And I called my shack "Break My Back,"
And the land was sweet and good,
And I did what I could.

Action Word Wheel Game

Directions:

1. Glue the Student Journal page to cardboard or heavy paper.
2. Cut out wheel and cover.
3. Fasten cover to wheel with brad or paper clip.
4. Spin the wheel to reveal an action word.
5. Act out the word for your group.

6. Have members guess which verb you are acting out.
7. Take turns selecting a word and guessing.
8. Challenge: Turn the wheel over and write your own words. Play the game again.

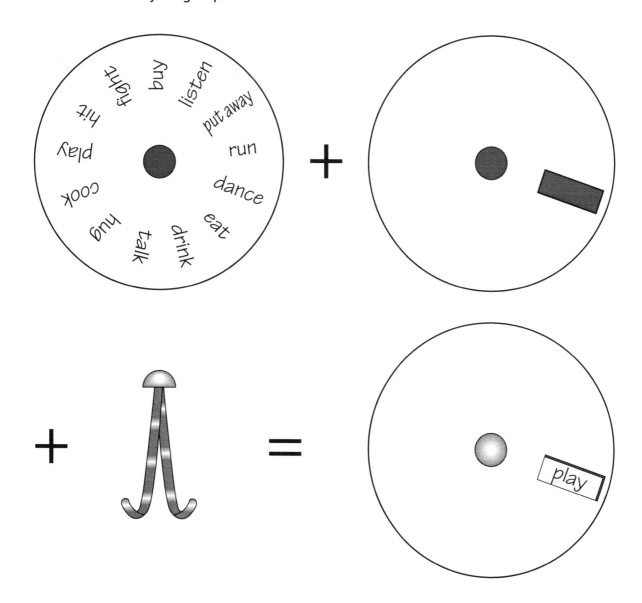

Use with student text page 36.

Pattern Hunt

1. Choose one of the patterns below.

Everybody loves _____ .

A _____ *is for* _____ .

2. Ask ten students to complete the pattern you choose.

_____

_____

_____

_____

_____

_____

_____

_____

_____

_____

3. Choose your favorite lines.
4. Arrange the lines into a poem in the box below.
5. Illustrate with your own drawings or pictures from magazines.

Use with student text page 38.

Word Data Base

A *data base* is a place to keep organized facts. You can make a data base on a chart or with a computer. To make a word data base, do the following:

1. Collect new words that you have learned during this unit.
2. Plan the information you want.
3. Use *fields* (special places for facts) such as the column headings below.

WORD DATA BASE					
Word	**Meaning**	**Sentence Using Word**	**Picture or Symbol**	**Pronunciation**	**Word Type**
shrug	move shoulders up	Mac shrugged his shoulders to tell us he didn't know the answer.		shrug	verb

(Activity Master 18)   Use with student text page 39.

Further Reading for Unit 1: Patterns

And the Green Grass Grew All Around: Folk Poetry from Everyone, collected by Alvin Schwartz. New York: HarperCollins Publishers, 1992. Folk poetry is poetry that people everywhere make up and pass on to others. This book includes great songs and poems about people, school, fun, stories, and many other topics. Many of the folk poems are funny.

Chicken Soup with Rice, by Maurice Sendak. New York: Scholastic, Inc., 1962. Sendak tells us what to do during each month of the year—and it always has something to do with chicken soup with rice. "I told you once/ I told you twice/all seasons of the year are nice/ for eating chicken soup with rice!"

Rise up Singing: The Group-Singing Song Book, edited by Peter Blood-Patterson. Bethlehem, PA: Sing Out Corporation, 1988. This book includes the words and chords to 1,200 songs! Some favorite "line story" songs are "The Green Grass Grows Around" (p. 169) and "The Old Woman Who Swallowed a Fly" (p. 171).

Talking to the Sun: An Illustrated Anthology of Poems for Young People, selected by Kenneth Koch and Kate Farrell. New York: Holt, Rinehart and Winston, 1985. This book has great poetry and great art, in categories like "All the Pretty Little Horses" and "A Rabbit as King of the Ghosts." The book includes some excellent concrete or "shape" poems.

'Til All the Stars Have Fallen, selections by David Booth. New York: Viking Penguin, 1989. David Booth, an education professor from Toronto, has collected (mostly) Canadian poems from many cultures, including some concrete or "shape" poems.

The Very Last First Time, by Jan Andrews. Buffalo, NY: Groundwood Books, 1985. This story takes place in a present-day Inuit community. When the tide is out in the winter, the Inuit people make holes in the ice and go under the ice to hunt for mussels. Part of growing up is doing this alone for the first time.

Where the Sidewalk Ends, poems and drawings by Shel Silverstein. New York: Harper and Row, 1974. Shel Silverstein never grew up. His poems and drawings are full of fun and silliness and thoughts about life from the point of view of young people.

Directions to the teacher:
Add your own recommendations to this list. Give copies to your school and community libraries so that they can acquire the books and/or make them available to students. Give copies to your students for suggested outside reading.

Use after Unit 1.

Write about a topic you choose.

_____

_____
_____
_____
_____
_____
_____
_____
_____
_____
_____
_____
_____
_____
_____
_____
_____
_____
_____
_____
_____

UNIT

2

Nature

(Activity Master 19)   *Use with student text page 42.*

Observing Nature with a Sense Chart

1. Sit alone outside to observe nature.
2. Write down on this chart what you see, hear, feel, smell, and taste in nature.
3. In the classroom, share and discuss with three other students what you observed.
4. On the back of this page, make a list of things you observed and how many people saw each of them.

SENSE CHART	
What do you see?	
What do you hear?	
What do you feel?	
What do you smell?	
What do you taste?	

(Activity Master 20)   *Use with student text page 47.*

What Comes in Threes?

What comes in groups of three in the poem "Three Sisters"?	What comes in groups of three in nature?

Use with student text page 48.

Mandala

A *mandala* is a symbol of the universe. It is a design in a circle shape.

Directions:
1. Draw a mandala with two parts on this sheet.
2. The two parts of the mandala show two contrasting pictures, for example, two sides of yourself.
3. Write about your mandala on the lines below.

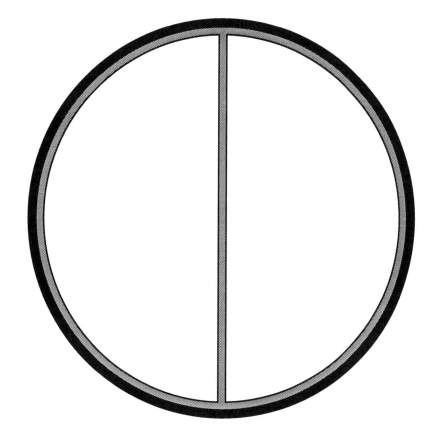

_____

_____

_____

_____

_____

_____

_____

Marking a Poem

Directions:
You will need three or four colors of pens or markers. You could also use different ways of marking: circling, underlining, putting in parentheses, underlining twice.

1. Choose one of the poems below.
2. Read the words once. Highlight any words that confuse or surprise you with one color. Check the meaning.
3. Read the poem a second time. In a second color, highlight words that show the most important ideas in the poem.
4. Read the poem a third time with a partner. As your partner reads the poem aloud to you, use a third color to highlight the words that your partner says louder or stronger when he or she reads it aloud.

Two Poems *by Dionne Brand*

Rain

It finally came
it beat on the house
it bounced on the flowers
it banged the tin roof
it rolled in the gutters
it made the street muddy
it spilled on the village
it licked all the windows
it jumped on the hill.
It stayed for two days
and then it left.

Hurricane

Shut the windows
Bolt the doors
Big rain coming
Climbing up the mountain.

Neighbors whisper
Dark clouds gather
Big rain coming
Climbing up the mountain.

Gather in the clotheslines
Pull down the blinds
Big wind rising
Coming up the mountain.

Branches falling
Raindrops flying
Tree tops swaying
People running
big wind blowing
Hurricane! on the mountain.

During other readings of the poem, you might look for and mark:
- Certain kinds of words (nouns, adjectives, verbs in the past or future tense, words relating to people or nature, etc.)
- A place in the poem where there is a change of mood or feeling
- Words that show *personification,* or giving human qualities to things

Word Squares

Directions:
1. Use the Word Squares to study new words.
2. Choose hard words from the poems on Student Journal #28.
3. Add other words you need to know.

Word: love	Sentence: I love my mother.	Word:	Sentence:
Meaning: a strong feeling of caring for someone else	**Symbol:**	**Meaning:**	**Symbol:**
Word:	**Sentence:**	**Word:**	**Sentence:**
Meaning:	**Symbol:**	**Meaning:**	**Symbol:**
Word:	**Sentence:**	**Word:**	**Sentence:**
Meaning:	**Symbol:**	**Meaning:**	**Symbol:**

Bringing Things to Life (Personification)

In "Rain," the poet speaks about rain as if it were alive. She writes, for example,

> *it licked all the windows*
> *it jumped on the hill.*

1. What animals or people act like "it" in the lines above?

2. Find more examples of poems that show weather acting like people or animals.

3. Share the lines of poetry you find with your classmates.

(Activity Master 25)   *Use with student text page 57.*

Cinquain

A *cinquain* is a kind of poem with five lines. Each line uses certain kinds of words.

Write a cinquain about an experience you have had of bad weather (or another topic you choose).
Share your writing with a classmate.

A cinquain has this form:

Line 1: a person, place, or thing (noun)
Line 2: two words that tell about the noun
Line 3: three *–ing* words that show action about the noun
Line 4: one four-word phrase or sentence about the noun
Line 5: the noun again (or a word that means the same)

Example:
Blizzard
White world
Snowing, blowing, freezing
Lost in empty space
Blizzard

Directions:
Use this format to write a cinquain.

_____

_____ _____

_____ _____ _____

_____ _____

_____

Use with student text page 57.

Quickwrite:
A Moment in Nature

1. Choose a moment in nature that you remember very well to write about.
2. Write about that moment on the lines below for a few minutes without stopping.
3. Share your ideas with a partner.
4. Talk about your partner's ideas. Tell your partner:

   • one thing you like
   • one thing you have more questions about
   • one suggestion for a change

_____

_____

_____

_____

_____

_____

_____

_____

_____

_____

_____

_____

_____

_____

_____

_____

_____

_____

Use with student text page 62.

Counting Syllables

Haiku are short poems that usually have 17 syllables. They often are about a season, and they use a surprising comparison from nature. They are sometimes arranged in three lines like this:

First line: 5 syllables
Second line: 7 syllables
Third line: 5 syllables

Count the syllables in each line of the haiku below. How many syllables are in each line? What are the patterns you find?

EXAMPLE:

	Syllables
Coming from the woods	5
A bull has a lilac sprig	7
Dangling from a horn	5

    —Richard Wright

At dawn

The pink clouds,   _____

Like hundreds of crabs,   _____

Creep from the hollows of heaven.   _____

    —Akiko Yosano

Come on, Owl!   _____

Come on, change that look of yours   _____

Now in the soft spring rain!   _____

    —Issa

Try to write your own haiku. What season will you write about? What will you compare? After you write the haiku, count the syllables you included in each line.

_____   _____

_____   _____

_____   _____

Use with student text page 62.

Contrast

Poets often use *contrast,* or comparing two people or things that are very different. Can you find two very different things or animals that are contrasted in each of the three haiku in the text? Can you find them in the haiku that you and your classmates wrote? Does the description make you think of something else? Try to fill in a chart the chart below with your answers. Discuss them with your class.

ELEMENTS OF HAIKU		
Author	**Two Things Contrasted**	**Makes Me Think of . . .**
EXAMPLE: Richard Wright	bull, lilacs	war and peace

Use with student text pages 63–64.

Cluster Map

1. Use a cluster map to organize words about a topic.
2. Put the most important words in the largest oval.
3. Put subcategories in the next size.
4. Put words that describe these subcategories in the smallest ovals.

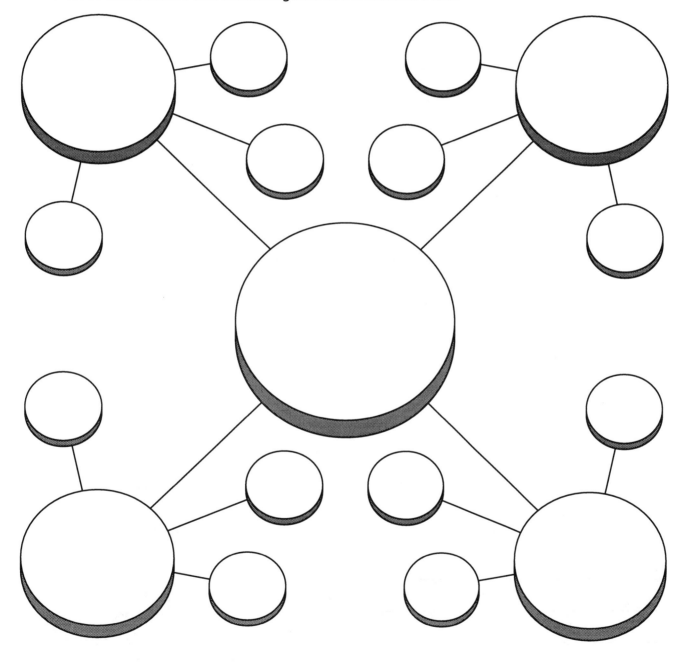

Use after student text page 63.

Write about a topic you choose.

Use with student text page 75.

Writing Dialogue

Rules for writing dialogue:

1. Use quotation marks before and after someone's exact words.

   "I had a dream."

2. Start a new line each time a different person speaks.

   "I had a dream."
   "What was your dream?"

3. Use a punctuation mark (. or ? or !) at the end of a sentence.

   "I had a dream."
   "What was your dream?"
   "I dreamed I won the lottery!"

4. Use a comma after the person talks if the sentence doesn't end.

   "If you won the lottery, buy me a new car," she said.

Writing a dialogue:

1. Talk to a small group of classmates about something you like to do.
2. Record your conversation with an audiocassette recorder.
3. Try writing down the words of two speakers in a short part of your tape.
4. See the example below.

   "What do you like to do?"
   "I like to climb rock walls."
   "Sounds scary. Where do you do that?"
   "Down on Mission Street in a big warehouse—or at Lake Tahoe."

Write your dialogue here:

_____

_____

_____

_____

_____

_____

_____

_____

Writing:
Writing Quotations, Writing an Ode

Write Quotations:

1. Write a short poem or story using dialogue.
2. Use quotation marks to show someone's exact words.
3. Start a new paragraph for each speaker.

_____

_____

_____

_____

_____

_____

_____

_____

_____

_____

Write an Ode:

1. Write a poem to someone or something you like a lot.
2. Address the person or thing, using "you."
3. Follow the pattern of "Ear of Corn" (Student Edition p. 67).

_____

_____

_____

_____

_____

_____

_____

_____

_____

(Activity Master 30)

Use with student text page 76.

Know/Want to Know/Learn Chart (K/W/L Chart)

1. Work in a small group.
2. In the first column (K) of the chart below, write things you *know* about rainforests.
3. In the second column (W) of the chart, write things you *want to know* about rainforests.
4. After you read and discuss "Saving the Rainforests," write down what you *learned* in the third column (L).

KNOW/WANT TO KNOW/LEARN CHART		
K	**W**	**L**

What Is a Rainforest?

Directions:

1. Work with a partner who has the chart **RAINFOREST FACTS B.** Each of you will have different information about rainforests.
2. You may not look at your partner's page.
3. Take turns asking your partner for information to complete your chart.
4. Write the questions and answers your partner tells you on your chart.
5. When you finish, each partner checks the other's chart.
6. Then quiz your partner on the information until he or she knows all the answers.

RAINFOREST FACTS A	
Where are the rainforests?	
	About 400 inches (1,024 cm) a year
What is the average temperature?	
	One season
What kinds of trees are there? How many different kinds are there?	
	125 species of mammals, 440 species of birds, 100 species of reptiles, 60 amphibians, 150 species of butterflies, and more other insects than you could ever count.
How many different species of flowering plants are there?	
	Very few people are left in the rainforest. They hunt and gather plants and fruits for food.

What Is a Rainforest?

Directions:

1. Work with a partner who has the chart **RAINFOREST FACTS A.** Each of you will have different information about rainforests.
2. You may not look at your partner's page.
3. Take turns asking your partner for information to complete your chart.
4. Write the questions and answers your partner tells you on your chart.
5. When you finish, each partner checks the other's chart.
6. Then quiz your partner on the information until he or she knows all the answers.

RAINFOREST FACTS B	
	Near the equator
How much rainfall is there in a year in a rainforest?	
	Average temperature is 80 degrees Fahrenheit (27 degrees centigrade)
How many seasons are there each year?	
	Most trees are evergreen. There are over 750 kinds of trees.
How many different species of animals are there?	
	1,500 species of flowering plants
Do people live in the rainforest? How do they live?	

(Activity Master 33)

Use with student text pages 79–80, 82.

Outlining Content-Area Text

Directions:
1. Read one paragraph of the selection below.
2. Write the main ideas in the left-hand column.
3. Write ideas that go with the main ideas (supporting ideas) in the right-hand column.

Saving the Rainforests

What would the world be like without trees? To find out, just hold your breath. Tropical rainforests are the "lungs" of the earth. They take carbon dioxide out of the air and give off oxygen for us to breathe. They also help keep the earth's temperature down. But people are destroying the rainforests. They are cutting down trees in order to survive.

Most rainforests are located in countries with little industry and growing populations. Cutting down trees is a way for poor people to make room for farms. The governments in those countries and companies from other countries also cut down trees for lumber and cattle ranches. The lumber, beef, and other products are sold in the U.S. and other countries.

But when a rainforest is destroyed, all the plants and animals that live there are destroyed, too. And the earth will heat up if there aren't enough trees to take carbon dioxide out of the air. Scientists call this *global warming*. It's a serious world problem.

What can be done? Can people in poor nations survive without cutting down their rainforests? Many say yes—but it will take a lot of planning and the help of other nations. The survival of the planet depends on it.

Main Ideas	Supporting Ideas
Paragraph 1: *We need trees to live.*	*Rainforests give off oxygen for us to breathe.*

Use with student text page 81.

Venn Diagram

Compare where you live with the rainforest on the Venn diagram.

1. In the "Rainforest" circle, write things that are true only about the rainforest.
2. In the "Where I Live" circle, write things that are true only about where you live.
3. In the place where the two circles overlap, write things that are true about both places.

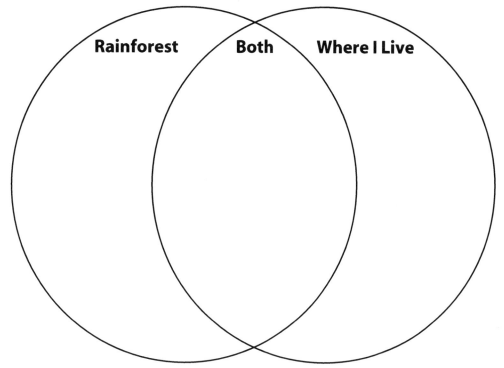

Rainforest   **Both**   **Where I Live**

4. When you have finished the Venn diagram, write about it on the lines below.

_____

_____

_____

_____

_____

_____

_____

Use with student text pages 82, 172.

Write a Letter

Use the format below to write a letter:

_____
(Date)

_____

_____
(Address of writer)

Dear _____,
(Salutation—"Dear [name of person you're writing to]")

_____

_____

_____

_____

_____

_____

_____

_____

_____

_____

Body (Use a paragraph for each main idea.)

_____,
(Closing—something like "Yours truly" or "Sincerely")

_____
(Signature of writer)

(Activity Master 38)

Use with student text page 83.

Further Reading for Unit 2: Nature

Fern Gulley: The Last Rainforest. Beverly Hills, CA: Fox Video, 1992. In this highly acclaimed fantasy film, an employee of a company that is cutting down the rainforest is changed by magical events. He works to overcome the evil power that's destroying the rainforest.

Grandfather's Dream, by Holly Keller. New York: Greenwillow Books, 1994. This book tells how a village in Vietnam successfully dammed part of the Mekong Delta so that the beautiful Sarus Cranes can roost in the area.

In a Spring Garden, edited by Richard Lewis. New York: Dial, no date. A delightful selection of spring haiku is illustrated with watercolor and collage by award-winning artist Ezra Jack Keats.

The Native Stories from Keepers of the Earth, by Michael J. Caduto and Joseph Bruchac. Los Angeles: First House Publisher, 1991. These 24 stories, collected from various Native North American groups, deal with the relationship of people to the earth. These stories can help us learn how to live with other creatures in harmony with nature.

The People Who Hugged the Trees, by Deborah Lee Rose. Niwat, CO: Roberts Rinehart, 1992. In this story from the state of Rajasthan in India, villagers hold a "sit-in" to stop a ruler from cutting down trees to build a new palace. The villagers rely on the grove of trees to protect them from desert storms.

Rain Forest, by Helen Cowcher. New York: Farrar Straus and Giroux, 1988. This book describes how the needs of animals living in the rainforests clash with what humans want. Machines cutting down the rainforest have threatened the centuries-old peaceful existence of the native plants and animals.

Tropical Rain Forest. Philadelphia: Coronet, 1989. This short video explores the many kinds of life in the tropical rain forest. Each layer of the forest provides its own separate habitat for plants and animals.

Welcome Back, Sun, by Michael Emberley. Boston: Little, Brown, 1993. A girl and her family who live in the mountains of Norway make their yearly walk up Mount Gusta to see the first rays of the sun in the spring.

The Year of the Panda, by Miriam Schlein. New York: HarperTrophy, 1992. This is the story of a Chinese boy who discovers a sick, abandoned panda bear. The boy seeks the help of a scientist from the United States to learn more about endangered species.

Directions to the teacher:

Add your own recommendations to this list. Give copies to your school and community libraries so that they can acquire the books and/or make them available to students. Give copies to your students for suggested outside reading.

Use after Unit 2.

Write about a topic you choose.

UNIT

3

Messages

(Activity Master 39)

Use with student text pages 86–87.

Brainstorm/Message Chart

1. Try to write all the ways you have seen people send and receive messages recently.
2. With your classmates, see how long a list you can make.
3. Use the chart to help you write information for the list.

MESSAGE			
Sender	**Receiver**	**Mode**	**Purpose**
Mom	Doctor	phone	to make an appointment
Minh	Maria	note	to find out if there's play practice

4. How many different modes or ways of sending messages did you find? _____

5. How many different purposes did you find? _____

6. What kinds of messages would you like to learn more about? _____

(Activity Master 40)

Use with student text page 92.

How are poems different from other kinds of writing?

There are many kinds of poems. Poems can tell stories or describe feelings or things that happen. How are poems different from other kinds of writing? One difference is how they look on the page.

1. Compare the poetry and prose below.
2. How do they look different?
3. Use the Venn diagram below to tell how the two texts are different and how they are the same.

It finally came,
it beat on the house
it bounced on the flowers
it banged the tin roof
it rolled in the gutters
it made the street muddy
it spilled on the village
it licked all the windows
it jumped on the hill.
It stayed for two days
and then it left.

What would the world be like without trees? To find out, just hold your breath. Tropical rainforests are the "lungs" of the earth. They take carbon dioxide out of the air and give off oxygen for us to breathe. They also help keep the earth's temperature down.

But people are destroying the rainforests. They are cutting down trees in order to survive.

Most rainforests are located in countries with little industry and growing populations. Cutting down trees is a way to make room for farms. The governments in those countries and companies from other countries also cut down trees for lumber and cattle ranches. Lumber, beef, and other products are then sold in the U.S. and other countries.

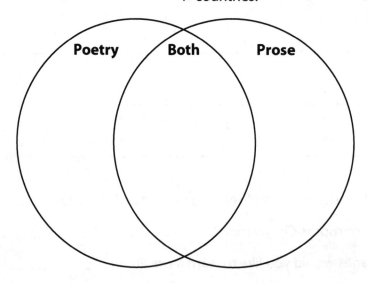

Poetry   **Both**   **Prose**

Writing Excuses

Write excuses for some of these situations. You can make them funny, serious, or both.

You don't have your homework.

You spilled water on someone in the cafeteria.

You missed an appointment.

You fell asleep in class.

You didn't finish your jobs at home.

Your socks don't match.

(Activity Master 41)   *Use with student text page 93.*

Think, Pair, Share

The chart below shows the steps of the Think–Pair–Share strategy.

THINK–PAIR–SHARE	
	THINK: Think about the topic. Write down notes.
	PAIR: Tell a partner about your ideas. Listen to your partner's ideas. Write down notes.
	SHARE: With your partner, join another pair. Each person shares his or her partner's ideas with the group of four.

Use Think–Pair–Share to think about and discuss a time someone told a secret.

1. ***Think.*** Think about that time. Who was it? What happened? How did you feel?

2. ***Pair.*** Share your thoughts with a partner. (You don't have to share the secret!)

3. ***Share.*** Get together with another pair of students. Take turns talking. Each person tells what his or her partner shared.

Use with student text page 100.

Keeping a Diary

Keep a diary telling something you did and/or thought about each day for a week:

Monday: _____
_____
_____
_____

Tuesday: _____
_____
_____
_____

Wednesday: _____
_____
_____
_____

Thursday: _____
_____
_____
_____

Friday: _____
_____
_____
_____

Saturday: _____
_____
_____
_____

Sunday: _____
_____
_____
_____

(Activity Master 42)   *Use with student text pages 101–104.*

Using Codes

Telephone Code:

1. Spell words by using the numbers and letters on each button of the dial.

2. A dot before the number (such as .2) means the first letter on the button.
   EXAMPLES: .8 = T
   .6 = M

3. A dot after the number (such as 2.) means the last letter on the button.
   EXAMPLES: 4. = I
   5. = L

4. A number with no dot means the middle letter on the button.
   EXAMPLES: 7 = R
   3 = E

Use telephone code to answer these questions.

Where do half of the world's plant and animal species live?
.8 7 6. .7 4. 2. .2 5. / 7 .2 4. 6 3. 6. 7 3 7. .8 7. / _____

How many syllables are in a haiku?
7. 3 8. 3 6 .8 3 3 6 _____

What is another name for a tornado?
.8 .9 4. 7. .8 3 7 _____

Write a secret message to a friend using telephone code.

(Activity Master 43)

Use with student text page 105.

Sunshine Outline

Use the Sunshine Outline below to summarize the story about the Navajo Code Talkers.

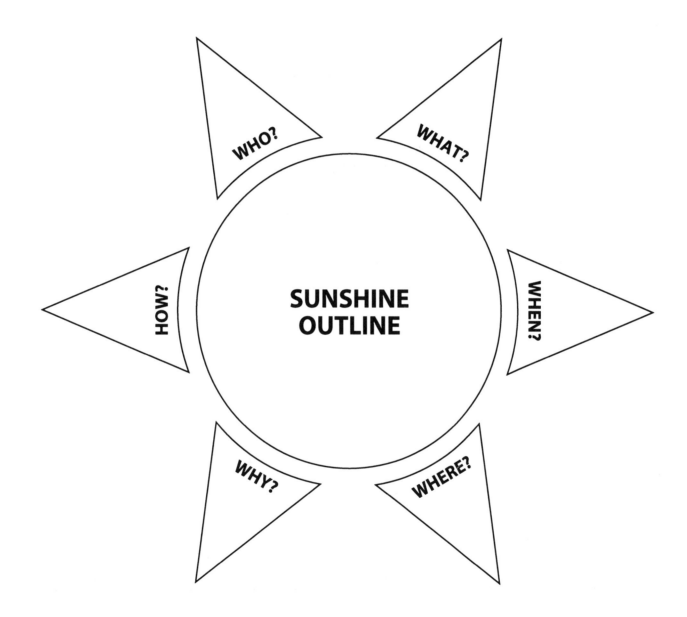

Sunshine Outline

Use the Sunshine Outline below to outline a story that really happened to you. Write the story on the lines below.

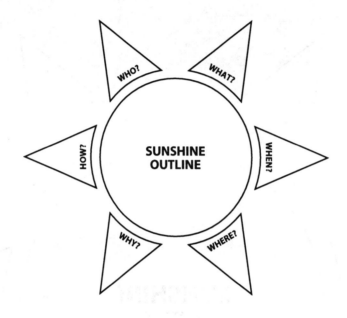

_____

_____

_____

_____

_____

_____

_____

_____

_____

_____

Use after student text page 106.

Write about a topic you choose.

_____

_____

_____

_____

_____

_____

_____

_____

_____

_____

_____

_____

_____

_____

_____

_____

_____

_____

_____

(Activity Master 44)

Use with student text page 107.

Being a Teenager

What are the hard things about being a teenager? What are the best things?

1. Work in a group of four.
2. Use the two-column chart below.
3. List the hard things in one column. List the best things in the other.

BEING A TEENAGER	
Best	**Hard**
Having friends	School
Don't have to pay rent	Not much money

Character Chairs

1. Label two chairs with the names of two characters in the play.
2. In groups of four, make a list of questions to ask the characters. Use the interview question starters below to help you think of questions.
3. Two people sit in the chairs and try to answer questions as if they were the characters. Write down some of the characters' answers.

Sample questions for Peter:

What do you think of Anne?
Why are you so quiet all the time?
Where do you want to go when you get out of the attic?

Interview Questions for _____
(your group's character's name)

1. **What do you think about** _____ ?

   Character's answer:

2. **Why do you** _____ ?

   Character's answer:

3. **Why are you so** _____ ?

   Character's answer:

4. **Where do you** _____ ?

   Character's answer:

5. **How did you know** _____ ?

   Character's answer:

6. **When did you** _____ ?

   Character's answer:

7. **What would you do if** _____ ?

   Character's answer:

(Activity Master 46)   *Use with student text page 117.*

Characters, Setting, and Plot

Characters are the people in a play.
The *setting* is the time when and the place where the play happens.
The *plot* is what happens.

Fill in the chart below, showing the characters, setting, and plot of each scene
in *The Diary of Anne Frank*.

Scene	Characters	Setting	Plot
1	Mr. Kraler Peter Mr. Frank Narrator Anne	The second floor of Mr. Kraler's office building, 1942	The Franks hide in the attic of the office building.
2			
3			
4			
5			
6			
7			

Roundtable Scene Writing

1. Work in a group of about four.
2. Decide where and when your scene will take place.
3. Each person chooses a character.
4. Decide what will happen in the scene.
5. Pass the page around the group. Each person writes his or her character's lines.
6. Each person makes a copy.
7. Read your scene out loud. Each person takes the part of the character he or she chose.

Title:

Where?

When?

Characters:

Dialogue:

_____

_____

_____

_____

_____

_____

_____

_____

_____

_____

_____

_____

_____

_____

(Activity Master 47)

Use with student text page 118.

Ranking Ladder

1. Use the ranking ladder to show which ideas or things are the most or least important.
2. Write one item on each line of the ladder.

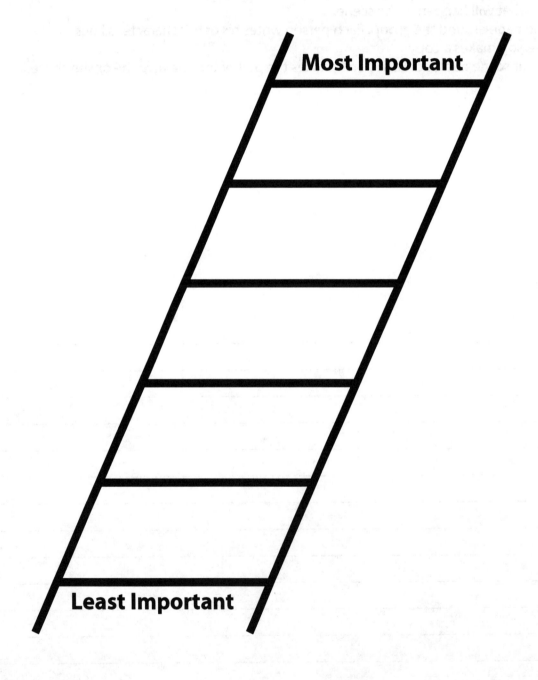

Most Important

Least Important

Compare and Contrast Messages

1. Choose two "messages" in selections from the unit that are very different from one another, for example, "This is just to say" and *The Diary of Anne Frank.*
2. Use the Venn diagram below to compare and contrast the two pieces.
3. Write about your comparison on the lines below.

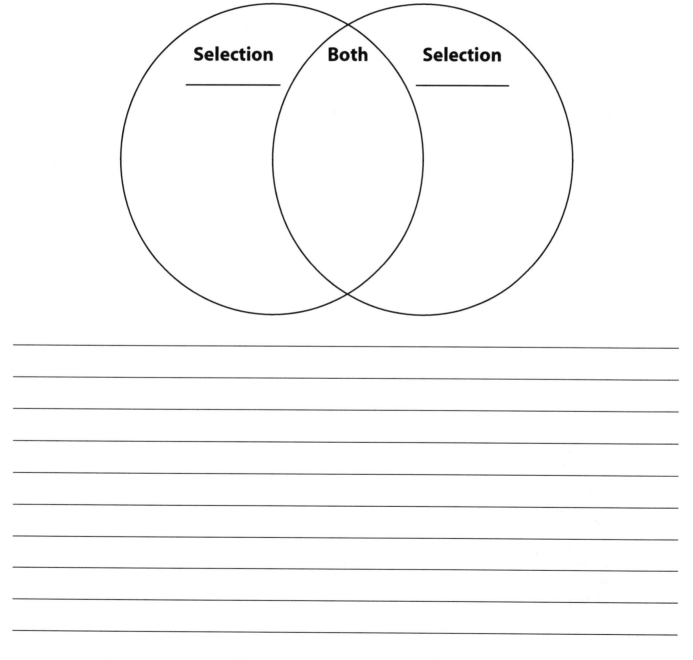

Selection   **Both**   **Selection**

_____   _____

(Activity Master 48) *Use as supplementary readings and activities for Unit 3.*

Rhythm

Rhythm is the pattern of soft and strong syllables. Poets use rhythm to make language interesting and easy to remember.

You can use marks to show rhythm:

4-Way Stop   Observe Speed Limit

Children Playing   Use Low Gear

Mark the rhythm in another stanza, or group of lines, in one of the poems below.

Traffic Signs: Two Found Poems

4-Way Stop, *by Myra Cohn Livingston*

4-Way Stop
No U-Turn
Observe Speed Limit
Railroad Crossing
Children Playing
Bridge Ahead
Use Low Gear
Watch Out for Deer
Curve Ahead
Left Lane Ends
Do Not Enter
Slippery When Wet
One-Way Street
Freeway Entrance
Last Stop for Gas
Do Not Pass
Come to a sign:
CAUTION—SLOW,
Who will stop?
Who will go?

Yield, *by Ronald Gross*

Yield.
No Parking.
Unlawful to Pass.
Wait for Green Light.
Yield.
Stop.
Narrow Bridge.
Merging Traffic Ahead.
Yield.
Yield.

Use with student text pages 120–121.

Further Reading for Unit 3: Messages

Anne Frank: The Diary of a Young Girl. New York: Random House, 1947. This is a translation of the diary Anne kept during World War II while she and her family were in hiding from the Nazis.

Anne Frank: Beyond the Diary: A Photographic Remembrance, by Rian van der Verhoeven. New York: Viking, 1993. Narration with quotations from Anne's diary accompanies photographs of her childhood, her years in the annex, and her life and death in a concentration camp.

Code Busters!, by Burton Albert, Jr. Niles, IL: Albert Whitman and Company, 1985. This book has code messages to solve that are written in dots and boxes, phone numbers, musical flags, and card decks.

Codes, Ciphers, and Other Secrets, by Karin N. Mango. New York: Franklin Watts, 1988. This book discusses secret languages and secret writing and includes codes from the past and the present.

The Collected Poems of William Carlos Williams, Volume I: 1909–1939, edited by A. Walton Litz and Christopher MacGowan. New York: New Directions, 1986. This volume includes almost 100 poems from the early part of Williams's career.

Communication, by Aliki. New York: Greenwillow, 1993. This book aims to help readers learn to express their feelings and to value what others say.

A Gathering of Days: A New England Girl's Journal, 1830–1832, by Joan W. Blos. New York, Scribner's, 1979. This is a fictional journal of a girl growing up in Maine in the 1830s. The girl reflects on an encounter with a runaway slave, the death of a friend, and her father's remarriage.

Letters from Rifka, by Karen Hesse. New York: Holt, 1992. In letters to her cousin in Russia, 12-year-old Rifka tells of her dangerous escape across the Russian border, her trip by sea to America, and her fears while being held in detention on Ellis Island.

Kinaalda: A Navajo Girl Grows Up, by Monty Roessel. Photographs and narrative tell the story of a Navajo girl who participates in the traditional coming-of-age ceremony of her people.

The Navajos, by Peter Iverson. New York: Chelsea House, 1990. This book gives a history of the Navajo people from the 1800s, when they first met white settlers, up to the present. It also includes pictures of Navajo silver and wool crafts.

"Navajo Code Talkers: A Few Good Men," by Bruce Watson. In *Smithsonian*, 24:5, pp. 34–45, August 1993. This article explains how the Code Talkers helped the Allied forces win World War II.

'Til All the Stars Have Fallen, selections by David Booth. New York: Viking Penguin, 1989. David Booth, an education professor from Toronto, has collected (mostly) Canadian poems from many cultures, including some concrete, or "shape" poems.

Voices and Visions: William Carlos Williams. New York Center for Visual History, 1988. This video is a collage of historical footage, interviews, animation, and dramatization about the poet's work.

Zlata's Diary: A Child's Life in Sarajevo, by Zlata Filipović. Translated by Christina Pribichevich-Zorich. New York: Viking Penguin, 1994. Zlata Filipović kept a diary of her life in Sarajevo, Bosnia. Before the war, she writes about her happy, normal life. Life changes in 1992—when her city is attacked—and her diary tells the very personal story of a child of war.

Directions to the teacher:

Add your own recommendations to this list. Give copies to your school and community libraries so that they can acquire the books and/or make them available to students. Give copies to your students for suggested outside reading.

Use after Unit 3.

Write about a topic you choose.

_____

UNIT

4

People

(Activity Master 51) *Use with student text page 124.*

World Map

Moving

1. Discuss with family members a time when you moved from one place to another.
2. Draw on the map below the route you took when you moved.
3. Work in small groups. Show your group where you lived before and after your move and the route you traveled.

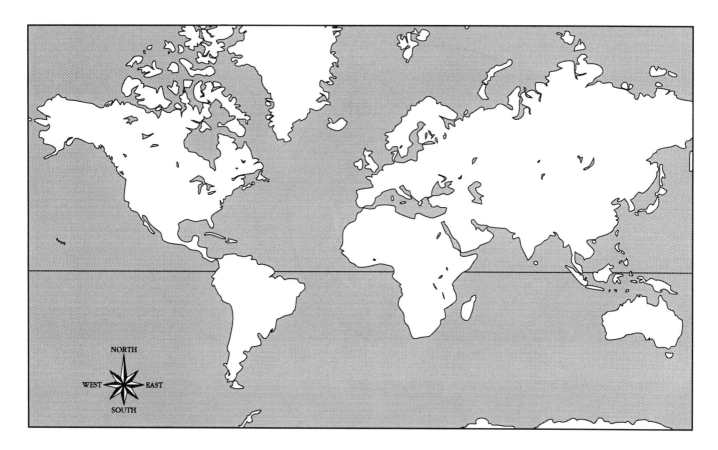

(Activity Master 52)   *Use with student text page 124.*

Venn Diagram:
Then and Now

A Venn diagram helps you compare two things.

1. Fill in the Venn diagram below to help you compare your life before and after you moved from one place to another.
2. Compare some of these things: school, neighborhood, friends, language, food, fun, house, transportation, and family.

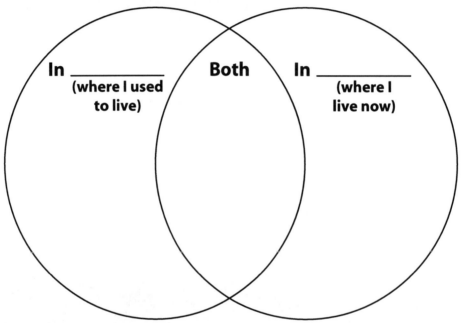

In _____
(where I used to live)

Both

In _____
(where I live now)

3. Write about your Venn diagram on the lines below.

_____

_____

_____

_____

_____

_____

_____

(Activity Master 53)

Use with student text pages 129–130.

Using Color to Show Moods

1. Read the poem "Miguel en el Norte" below. Think about what moods the poet expresses in his poem.
2. In the box below, make a key for colors that express different moods to you. Tell a partner what mood each color shows.
3. Use colored pencils or markers to underline each part of the poem. Mark the part of the poem with the color of the mood the words make you feel.
4. Tell your partner why you used the colors you did.
5. Discuss with the class what you think are the moods of this poem.

Color	Mood

Miguel en el Norte, *by Jorge Argueta*

In El Salvador
Miguel's life
was one of
mangos, guayabas, and nizperos,
starry nights,
rivers filled with nests,
and green meadows
to run through with joy.

But one day Miguel
was forced to leave
his country.
He fled to the North,
where everything is cold and foggy,
and they speak English.

But Miguel doesn't speak
any English.
He can say
hi, yes, bye, and no,
but that's about it.

Miguel is sad.
He yearns for
the mango trees,
the guayabas,
the nizperos,
and the green meadows
to run through with joy.

Revising and Editing a Poem

1. Use the ideas on the Venn diagram you made (student text p. 124, Activity Master 52, Student Journal #66) to plan a poem about a time when you moved.
2. Write sense words about the two places you have lived on the chart below. Use a thesaurus or translation dictionary to help find new words. Underline the words in a color that shows their mood or tone.

FIVE SENSES CHART				
Find words related to the ways you sense things.				
See	**Hear**	**Feel**	**Taste**	**Smell**

3. Write the poem with colored markers or pencils that show your moods.
4. Share your draft with a classmate. Revise, edit, and share with the whole class.

Your Poem

_____

_____

_____

_____

_____

_____

_____

_____

_____

_____

Example *by Nasir*

In Pakistan
Nasir's life
was one of
rice and chicken,
flying kites, and
playing croquet
with Fraba and Fraidoon
Shakela and Shekaba.

(Activity Master 55)

Use with student text page 131.

Drawing and Writing About a Family Gathering

1. What do families like to do together? Share ideas.
2. Draw a picture of your family doing something you like to do together.
3. Label all the people and things in the picture.
4. Tell a partner about your picture.
5. Write about the picture on the lines below. Use the words in your labels.

(Activity Master 56)   *Use with student text pages 132–139.*

Who's Doing What?

1. Choose some individual people to study in the O'Kelley painting on p. 132 and the Garza painting on p. 136.
2. Reread the texts that go with the paintings.
3. Use the chart below to describe what you have learned.
4. Share and discuss your chart with classmates.

WHO IS DOING WHAT?				
Who did you study?	**What is the person doing?**	**Did you find out from the text or the picture or both?**	**Is this person in the O'Kelley or Garza captioned picture?**	**Would you like to do this? Why or why not?**
Man in mustache (grandpa?)	soaking corn husks	both	Garza	Yes. I'd like to do it so I could eat the tamales.

(Activity Master 58)

Use with student text page 140.

Writing Description

Writers make their writing interesting and colorful by their use of description. They write so that you can picture in your mind what they write about. They choose interesting facts to share with the reader.

1. Use a family photograph, draw a picture of your family, use your picture from Activity Master 55, or choose a picture of a family from your *Voices* text or a magazine.
2. Label all the people and things in the picture. Look up the words you don't know. Use a picture dictionary or translation dictionary.
3. Label the feelings you think the people in the picture are feeling.
4. Write about your picture. Use the words in your label and caption.
5. Read your writing and/or tell the class about your picture. Try to include some interesting facts in your description.
6. Revise your writing and add a page with your picture.

_____

_____

_____

_____

_____

Write about a topic you choose.

(Activity Master 59)

Use with student text page 141.

Brave People Hunt

1. Think about someone brave. What are three words that describe this person? What brave thing did the person do? Write the answers on the chart below.
2. Ask other people in your class about the brave person they know about. Write their answers on your chart.
3. Make a class list of brave people and the words that describe them.

BRAVE PEOPLE HUNT				
Name of class member	Name of brave person	How you know about the person	Three words that describe the person	Something brave the person did and why
Mia	Martin Luther King	TV, my mom, books	non-violent, minister, leader	led a bus strike so people could sit where they wanted

(Activity Master 60)   *Use with student text page 145.*

Point-of-View Chart

1. Use the chart below to plan questions for characters in the story of Harriet Tubman.
2. Students stand in front of the class. Each person plays the part of one point of view.
3. Class members ask them questions.
4. Characters answer the questions from their points of view.

POINT OF VIEW	
Harriet Tubman 1. Why did you run away? 2. Why did you go back? 3.	**Slave Owner** 1. How do you feel about owning another human being? 2. 3.
Tree in the Forest 1. How did you help Harriet and her friends? 2. 3.	**Slave Catcher** 1. Why were you a slave catcher? 2. 3.
People Who Helped in the Underground Railroad 1. 2. 3.	**People Whom Harriet Helped to Escape** 1. 2. 3.

Story Sequence Outline

Narrative Poem or Prose Activity Master

You can tell a story with poetry or prose. In the poem "Harriet Tubman," Eloise Greenfield tells the true story of a woman who ran away from slavery and then returned to help others run away.

1. Use the story sequence outline below to outline your own story.
2. You may choose to write about the brave person you thought of in the "Brave People Hunt" activity. Use your notes on the chart from student text p. 141 or Activity Master 59.
3. Using your outline, tell a partner about your story.
4. Ask your partner questions about his or her story.
5. Write your story as prose or a poem. Illustrate it, if you like.

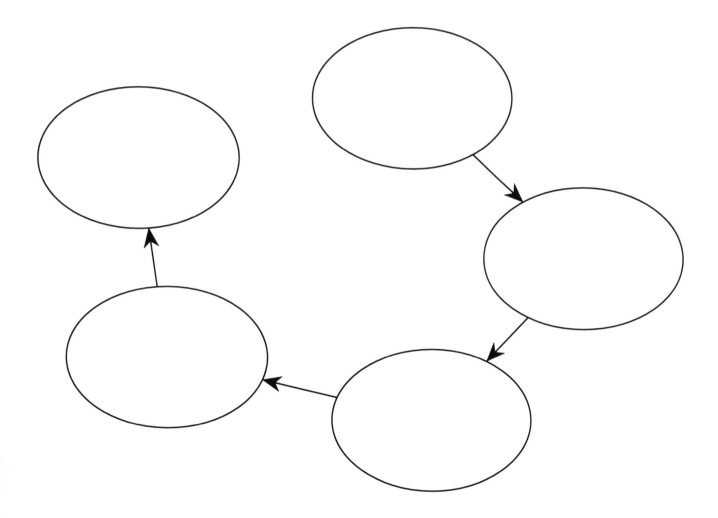

Use with student text page 146.

Story Map

Playing a Trick

Do you know of a story (real or not) in which people get what they want by playing a trick?

1. Make a story map of your story.
2. Fill in the boxes with pictures and/or words.
3. Use your map to help you share your story with classmates.

1. Character and setting	2. Initial event	3. Goal setting
4. Attempts to reach goal	5. Results	6. Resolution of problem

Use with student text page 146.

Writing a Narrative

1. Write the story of the brave person you thought about for the "Brave People Hunt" activity.
2. Use a Story Sequence Outline (Activity Master 61, Student Journal #75) or Story Map (Activity Master 62, Student Journal #76) to outline your story.
3. Use your outline to help you write the story below.
4. Read your story to a partner.
5. Use "EQS" (see Student Journal #94) to offer one another encouragement and suggestions.

_____

_____

_____

_____

_____

_____

_____

_____

_____

_____

_____

_____

_____

_____

_____

_____

_____

_____

(Activity Master 63)

Use with student text pages 154, 156.

Open Mind Diagram

1. Work in small groups.
2. Each group chooses one of the characters from "The Fly": the usurer, the child, or the mandarin.
3. Use the "Open Mind" diagram below to describe your character's thoughts. Use a dictionary, translation dictionary, or thesaurus to help you find the best words.
4. Share your diagram with the class.

Writing Dialogue

A *dialogue* is a short part of a play with two people.

1. Work in pairs to write a dialogue that tells a story.
2. Each person writes in one column below.
3. Each person takes the part of one person in the dialogue and writes the "lines" of that person in one column.
4. Take turns writing lines. Help your partner when it is his or her turn. Try to make something in your dialogue surprising.
5. Read your dialogue for the class.

Character 1:	Character 2:
1	
	2
1	
	2
1	
	2
1	
	2

Further Reading for
Unit 4: People

From the Hills of Georgia, by Mattie Lou O'Kelley. Boston: Atlantic Monthly Press, 1983. Mattie Lou O'Kelley drew from her experiences of growing up on a farm in the southern United States to create these 28 bright and colorful folk paintings.

Mattie Lou O'Kelley: Folk Artist. Boston: Little, Brown, 1989. O'Kelley's paintings feature scenes of animals, people, and activities during all four seasons.

Harriet Tubman and the Underground Railroad. New York: McGraw-Hill, 1964. This film dramatizes the 19 trips Harriet Tubman made into slave territory between 1850 and 1860.

Honey, I Love, by Eloise Greenfield. New York: Harper Trophy, 1978. Greenfield's poetry looks at life as seen by a young girl. In these 16 poems, she talks about riding on a train, playing games with her friends, and sharing love with her family. This collection includes the poem "Harriet Tubman."

Family Pictures, by Carmen Lomas Garza. San Francisco: Children's Book Press, 1990. A famous Mexican American painter uses words and pictures to share her childhood memories of growing up in a Hispanic community in southern Texas. The author deals with everyday experiences like picking oranges as well as special activities such as going to a Mexican fair.

Favorite Folktales from Around the World, edited by Jane Yolen. New York: Pantheon Books, 1986. This book, which includes "The Fly," collects witty, wise, and scary stories from many different countries in Asia, Europe, and North America. It includes sections of tales about heroes, fools, shape shifters, and ghosts.

The Land I Lost: Adventures of a Boy in Vietnam, by Huynh Quang Nhoung. New York: Harper and Row, 1986. The author shares amazing and exciting childhood adventures of village life in Vietnam before the Vietnam War.

The Season of Secret Wishes, by Iva Prochazkova. New York: Lothrop, Lee & Shepard, 1989. Kapka is an 11-year-old girl living in Czechoslovakia right before the country becomes a democracy. After Kapka's father is turned away from a government-sponsored art show, he gets in trouble with the officials for displaying his sculptures in a private street exhibition.

Directions to the teacher:
Add your own recommendations to this list. Give copies to your school and community libraries so that they can acquire the books and/or make them available to students. Give copies to your students for suggested outside reading.

Use after Unit 4.

Write about a topic you choose.

UNIT

5

Peace

(Activity Master 66) *Use with student text page 160.*

Concentric Circles Chart

1. Fill in the concentric circles chart below. Name the places where you live, for example:

    Planet: *Earth*

2. Write about a peaceful situation in this place inside the ring, for example:

    Earth — There is no more war anywhere on Earth.

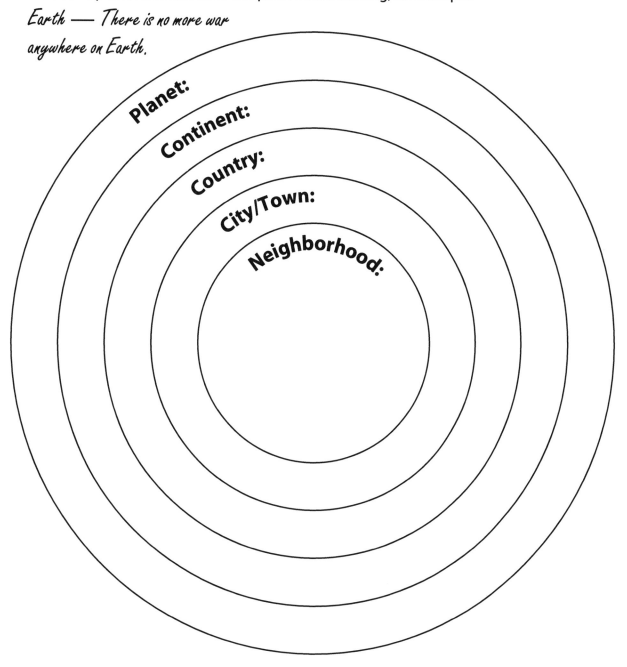

Finding a Win–Win Solution

1. Work with a partner.
2. Discuss one of the problems below, or make up your own conflict situation.
3. Add more details to the story. Try to find a solution in which both people win.
4. Write your answer on chart paper or on the board.
5. Read everyone's answers and discuss. Write the win–win solutions below.

    A. A student is sitting in the best seat on the bus.
        Another student comes up and says, "You're sitting in my seat!"

        Win–Win Solution:

    B. As a joke, a student takes another student's backpack and hides it.
        The student whose backpack has been stolen doesn't think it's funny.

        Win–Win Solution:

    C. Two students talk about a third student behind his or her back.
        The third student finds out and is angry.

        Win–Win Solution:

    D. A teacher accuses a student of cheating on a test.
        Another student saw that the student did not cheat.

        Win–Win Solution:

    E. A sister and brother want to watch different TV shows.
        They have only one TV.

        Win–Win Solution:

    F. Two students are doing layout for the yearbook together.
        One student keeps forgetting meetings. The other feels that he or she is doing all the work.

        Win–Win Solution:

    G. A group of students fills a table in the cafeteria.
        Another student wants to join them.

        Win–Win Solution:

Use with student text page 166.

Write About a Choice

1. Write below about a choice you have had or that you might have.
2. Write so that your reader can see a picture.
3. Don't tell which choice you made. Let your reader make his or her own choice.
4. Exchange journals with a partner. Read and discuss.

_____

_____

_____

_____

_____

_____

_____

_____

_____

_____

_____

_____

_____

_____

_____

_____

_____

_____

_____

_____

Problem-Solving Wheel

This problem-solving wheel shows the different ways that problems between people can be solved.

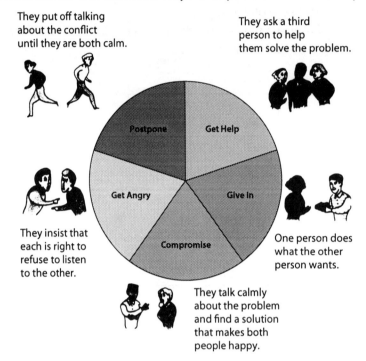

They put off talking about the conflict until they are both calm.

They ask a third person to help them solve the problem.

They insist that each is right to refuse to listen to the other.

One person does what the other person wants.

They talk calmly about the problem and find a solution that makes both people happy.

1. Look at the solutions you and your classmates found for the problems on Activity Master 67.

2. Which part of the wheel shows how each problem was solved? _____
   _____

3. Think of a conflict that you have had with another person. Write it on the lines below.
   _____
   _____
   _____

4. How did you resolve the problem? _____
   _____
   _____
   _____

5. Which part of the wheel shows the way you resolved the problem?
   _____

Characteristics of a Good Speech Chart

1. Look back at the speech of Chief Joseph.
2. Can you find the characteristics of a good speech?
3. Use the chart to help you.

CHARACTERISTICS OF A GOOD SPEECH	
Characteristic	**Examples in Chief Joseph's Speech**
Short, clear sentences	
Simple, clear structure	
Strong, memorable words	
Other	

Use with student text page 172.

Write a Letter for Change

Use the format below to write a business letter to help cause a change.

_____

(Date)

_____

_____

(Address of writer)

Dear _____:

(Salutation—"Dear [name of person you're writing to]:")

Body (Use a paragraph for each main idea.)

_____

_____

_____

_____

_____

_____

_____

_____

_____

_____

_____

_____,

(Closing—something like "Yours truly" or "Sincerely")

_____

(Signature of writer)

Write about a topic you choose.

_____

_____

_____

_____

_____

_____

_____

_____

_____

_____

_____

_____

_____

_____

_____

_____

_____

(Activity Master 70)   *Use with student text page 177.*

Fishbone Outline

1. Work in a small group.
2. Write what happened in the poem on the fishbone outline below.
3. Write the final result on the fish head.

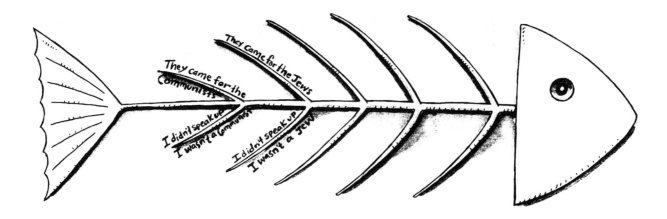

They came for the Jews

They came for the Communists

I didn't speak up
I wasn't a Communist

I didn't speak up
I wasn't a Jew

4. Discuss/write:

   • Can you think of other situations like this one? _____

   _____

   _____

   _____

   _____

   • What do you think is the main idea of this poem? _____

   _____

   _____

   _____

   _____

(Activity Master 71)
Use with student text page 178.

On Speaking Up for Each Other

The writer of this poem used a structure, or plan, that makes the writing make sense. This structure helps the poem hold together and be powerful just as bone structure holds a fish together.

1. Underline the words in each stanza that are the same.

On Speaking Up for Each Other
by Martin Niemöller (1892–1984)

In Germany they came first for the Communists,
and I didn't speak up
because I wasn't a Communist.

Then they came for the Jews,
and I didn't speak up
because I wasn't a Jew.

Then they came for the trade unionists,
and I didn't speak up
because I wasn't a trade unionist.

Then they came for the Catholics,
and I didn't speak up
because I was a Protestant.

Then they came for me,
and by that time
no one was left to speak up.

2. How are the first lines of each stanza the same? _____

_____

3. When do they change? _____

_____

4. Can you tell about, or make a picture of, the structure of the poem? _____

_____

_____

(Activity Master 72)

Use with student text page 178.

Time Sequence Story Map

Use the following structure to plan a selection of your own. You may choose to write about a time when you needed help and someone helped you or no one helped you.

TIME SEQUENCE STORY MAP
First...
Then...
Then...
Then...
Finally...

(Activity Master 73)   *Use with student text page 183.*

Comparing and Contrasting with a Chart

Use the chart below to compare and contrast the experiences of Zlata Filipović and Anne Frank.

COMPARING AND CONTRASTING ZLATA FILIPOVIĆ AND ANNE FRANK			
TOPIC	Zlata	Anne	Both
Where she lived			
When she lived			
Her family			
How she spent time at home			
What the war was about			
Other:			
Other:			

Use with student text pages 194–195.

Further Reading for Unit 5: Peace

Chief Joseph: Nez Percé Leader, by Marian W. Taylor. New York: Chelsea House, 1993. Chief Joseph bravely resisted the U.S. government and led his people toward a safer home. The Nez Percé traveled over 1,800 miles until they finally had to surrender near Canada.

The Declaration of Human Rights, adapted by Ruth Rocha and Octavio Roth. United Nations Publications, 1989. Octavio Roth's prints illustrate the text included in this unit.

A Hand Full of Stars, by Rafik Schami. (Translated by Rika Lesser.) New York: Dutton, Puffin, 1989. An Arab teen in Damascus writes in his journal about himself, his family, and his friends in a war-torn country.

Honey and Salt, by Carl Sandburg. New York: Harcourt Brace Jovanovich, 1963. These 77 poems, published when Sandburg was 85 years old, ask important questions on themes of life and love.

I Dream of Peace, compiled by UNICEF. New York: HarperCollins, 1994. Writings and drawings by children from the former Yugoslavia vividly reveal the pain and suffering caused by war in their homeland. This book cries for an end to the fighting.

The Nez Percé, by Virginia Driving Hawk Sneve. New York: Holiday House, 1994. Historical photographs and paintings help the author tell about the customs and everyday life of the Nez Percé tribe. Europeans gave the Nez Percé (literally, "pierced nose") their name from their custom of wearing ornaments in their noses.

The Nez Percé, by Clifford E. Trafzer. New York: Chelsea House, 1992. This book includes a history of the Nez Percé from the early 1800s, when they first began trading with white settlers, to their present-day life.

Peace Begins with You, by Katherine Scholes. New York: Little, Brown, 1989. This book explains how and why peace has a place in all of our lives. It addresses national and international issues of peace, including environmental ones.

A Picture Book of Rosa Parks, by David A. Adler. New York: Holiday House, 1993. Robert Casilla's soft-edged color paintings illustrate the story of Rosa Parks's role in the Civil Rights movement in the U.S. in the 1950s.

Rise up Singing, edited by Peter Blood-Patterson. Bethlehem, PA: Sing-Out, 1988. Words and chords for over 2,000 songs provide a great source for fun and language learning. Peace songs have their own section, on pp. 158–166.

Rose Blanche, by Roberto Innocenti. Mankato, Minnesota: Creative Education, 1985. During World War II, a young German girl discovers children held as prisoners in a Nazi concentration camp near her home. She helps keep them alive by secretly bringing them food.

Wind Song, by Carl Sandburg. New York: Harcourt Brace and Company, 1960. The poet wrote these 100 poems especially for young readers. Titles include "Buffalo Bill," "Little Girl Be Careful What You Say," and "Frog Songs."

A World in Our Hands: In Honor of the Fiftieth Anniversary of the United Nations. Berkeley, CA: Ten Speed Press, 1995. To celebrate the golden anniversary of the United Nations, students aged 7–21 from 115 countries created and edited this history of the organization. The book includes painting, photography, writing, and poetry that explore issues young people care about and paint a vision of the future as they see it.

Directions to the teacher:

Add your own recommendations to this list. Give copies to your school and community libraries so that they can acquire the books and/or make them available to students. Give copies to your students for suggested outside reading.

Write about a topic you choose.

_____

_____

_____

_____

_____

_____

_____

_____

_____

_____

_____

_____

_____

_____

_____

_____

_____

_____

_____

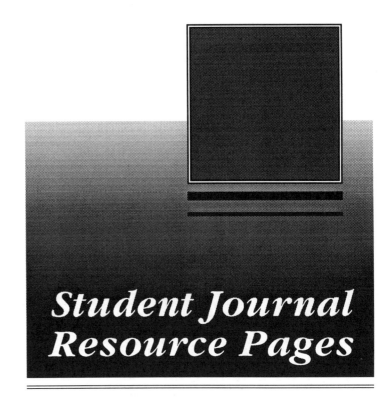

Student Journal Resource Pages

These pages of the Student Journal are placed together in the back of the book. You will be able to find them easily and use them many times.

(Activity Master 11)

Use with any process writing activity.

Steps in the Writing Process

1. Prewriting

Think about your writing, gather ideas and information, and make plans. You might use:

A Story Map
A Character Web
A Cluster Chart
A Venn Diagram

2. Drafting

Get your ideas down on paper. Try to write quickly and fluently, and not to worry now about details like spelling and punctuation. Try a quickwrite.

3. Sharing

Share your writing with a partner or small group. When you respond to others' writing, remember:

First, offer encouragement and tell them the parts you like.
Second, ask questions to help the writer come up with more information or ideas.
Third, offer suggestions for improving or polishing the writing.

4. Revising

After you get ideas and suggestions from your peers and your teacher, add needed information, delete unnecessary information, clarify details, improve word choices, and organize the piece.

5. Editing

Use an Editing Checklist to check your own work for improvements needed in spelling, usage, punctuation, arrangement of words on the page, etc. You might like to trade papers with a partner and proof one another's work.

6. Publishing

Share your work with the world! Here are some ways to publish:

- *Put it in a book in the class or school library.*
- *Read it aloud to the class.*
- *Post it on the wall in the classroom or hall.*
- *Read it to the school on a video broadcast.*
- *Make an accordion book.*
- *Send it through E-mail.*
- *Submit it to the school paper or literary magazine.*

(Activity Master 17)

Use after group activities.

Group Activity Evaluation

Date:

Name:

Activity:

MY CONTRIBUTIONS		
Added ideas to the project	☐ Yes ☐ No	***Examples:***
Worked well with other group members	☐ Yes ☐ No	***Examples:***
Contributed fair share of work	☐ Yes ☐ No	***Examples:***
Took leadership roles	☐ Yes ☐ No	***Examples:***
Encouraged other group members	☐ Yes ☐ No	***Examples:***
Other:	☐ Yes ☐ No	***Examples:***

How well did your whole group work together?

_____

_____

_____

_____

_____

_____

(Activity Master 35) *Use with any process writing activity.*

Responding to Peers' Writing: EQS

E: Encourage	Q: Ask Questions	S: Suggestions
Help your partner know what he or she is doing right. 　Be specific. *"I liked the surprise at the end the best."* *"You used some very interesting words in this sentence."* *"This poem made me think about my homeland."*	Ask questions when you would like more information. 　Ask questions when something isn't quite clear. *"Why did your grandmother give you that picture?"* *"What do you mean, 'He went back'? Where did he go?"*	Ask your partner if he or she would like some suggestions. 　If your partner says "Yes," offer suggestions to make the writing better. 　Always let your partner choose whether or not to use your ideas. 　Let your partner own his or her writing. *"You might try saying 'My dog is fat' another way. How about 'My dog looks like a sausage with four legs'?"* *"What if you changed these two sentences around?"*

Read your partner's selection. Use EQS to fill in the boxes.

Name: _____ **Partner's Name:** _____

(Activity Master 37)

Use with any process writing activity.

Editing Checklist #1

Name _____ **Date** _____

Title _____

EDITING CHECKLIST 1		
Edit for Mechanics:	✔	**Comments**
Information • Did I write my name, date, and title on the page?	☐	
Form • Did I indent the first line of each paragraph lIke this? _____ _____ _____	☐	
Capitals • Did I capitalize names of people and special places? • Did I start every sentence with a capital letter?	☐ ☐	
Other: • • •	☐ ☐ ☐	

(Activity Master 49)   *Use with any process writing activity.*

Editing Checklist #2

Name _____   **Date** _____

Title _____

EDITING CHECKLIST 2		
Edit for Correct Use of Words:	✔	**Comments**
Spelling • Did I check all the words I wasn't sure about?	☐	
• If I used a word processor, did I use spell check?	☐	
• Did I ask a friend to double-check my spelling?	☐	
Word Choice • Did I choose interesting words?	☐	
• Did I use a thesaurus or dictionary to help me choose better words?	☐	
• Did I use strong verbs? (Hint: When I can, I should change forms of "to be" to other, more active verbs.)	☐	
Other: •	☐	
•	☐	
•	☐	

STUDENT JOURNAL #97

(Activity Master 57)   Use with student text page 140 and other writing activities.

Editing Checklist #3

Name _____   **Date** _____

Title _____

EDITING CHECKLIST 3		
Edit for Correct Use of Words:	✔	**Comments**
Grammar and Usage • Does my writing make sense? Did I ask a classmate to read it to check?	☐	
• Are my sentences complete? Do they have a subject and a verb?	☐	
• Did I punctuate each sentence with the right mark ("." or "!" or "?")?	☐	
• Is my writing all in the same tense (for example, present or past)?	☐	
• Did I use pronouns "she," "her," or "hers" for women and girls and "he," "him," or "his" for men and boys?	☐	
• Did I use singular pronouns for one person or thing and plural pronouns for more than one?	☐	
• Do my verbs match my subjects? Do I use singular verbs with one subject, plural verbs with more than one?	☐	
Other: •	☐	
•	☐	
•	☐	

Editing Checklist #4

Name _____   **Date** _____

Title _____

EDITING CHECKLIST 4		
Edit for Composition:	✔	**Comments**
Organization • How is my work organized?	☐	
• Is my plot or other organization clear and logical? Did I ask a peer to read it to check?	☐	
Beginning • Do I have a strong, interesting beginning that makes the reader want to keep reading?	☐	
Ending • Do I have a strong ending that makes the reader remember my writing?	☐	
Sentences • Did I use different kinds of sentences and words to make my writing interesting?	☐	
Other: •	☐	
Other: •	☐	